Contents

Increasing Reading Power

Reading novels provides us with opportunities to reflect on human behaviors, emotions, values, relationships, and conflicts. When we read a novel, we are invited to step outside our own lives and to become spectators observing imaginary events that might or might not occur in real life. At the same time, we become participants in these events as we are drawn into the story and share the feelings and experiences of the characters.

As we develop our lives as readers – and this is a lifelong process – we come to appreciate a story not only by identifying with the characters but also by seeing through the eyes of the author. In reading and responding to novels, we become aware of how an author uses his or her talents and skills to create stories. We learn to note the author's choices in terms of style, language, action, and characters. As we read, we rewrite the novel in our minds. We reflect on our interaction with the text and make connections to our personal library of literary experiences.

We can increase our reading power through intensive and extensive experiences with novels. Readers can choose from a vast range of novels written by many fine authors. We can take countless imaginary journeys involving characters and situations that may be familiar or completely new. Novels can provide road maps that help us cope with life's difficulties.

In the classroom, we can explore novels that have been read as a class or by a group, that explore a theme, or that have been read aloud. As well, we can explore response activities that prepare readers for a novel, that accompany the reading of a novel, or that help us to reflect on a novel. Novels contain a wealth of stories. Response activities will lead to dozens more.

Thinking About…Reading Novels

- What can we learn by reading novels?
- How is reading a novel different from other reading?

Reflecting on Our Reading

To understand ourselves as readers, it's important to think about what we read and how we read. Everyone has different attitudes, feelings, and interests related to reading. You can reflect on yourself as a reader:

1. at the beginning of the school year to determine your interests and needs;
2. during the year to determine progress, changes in attitudes, and goal-setting; and
3. at the end of the year to identify successes, challenges, and growth in your reading behaviors and abilities.

As part of your reflection, you might choose to:
- complete an independent self-assessment profile;
- participate in an interview with a teacher or a parent/guardian; or
- work with a partner or in a small group to share and discuss answers to the reading questionnaire shown here.

Reading Questionnaire
1. Are you a good reader? How do you know?
2. What books did you read when you were younger?
3. How did you learn to read?
4. Is reading important to you outside of school?
5. What do you do well as a reader?
6. What kinds of activities help you to understand what you are reading?
7. What might you like to change about your reading habits?
8. Why do you think people read novels?
9. How do you decide what novels to read?
10. What do you do when you have difficulty reading a novel?

Thinking About...Your Life as a Reader

- How would you describe yourself as a reader?
- What do you like to read? Why?
- What are some challenges that you experience as a reader?
- What goals might you set to improve your reading?

1. WHY READ NOVELS?

Three Ways to Organize a Novel Program

Whole Class   This approach to reading can take two forms:

1. All students experience the same novel.
2. The teacher reads a novel aloud to the whole class.

In option 2, teachers introduce students to material they might never read on their own. They help students discover new genres, authors, series of novels, worldviews, and cultures. Listening to a good novel read aloud one section at a time can connect students to a theme or themes that they can discuss and explore in depth. By modeling fluency and engagement in a read aloud, teachers demonstrate the pleasures of reading and the satisfaction of a story well told. Books that are slightly above most students' reading abilities are most appropriate for a read aloud.

Small Groups   Commonly, teachers form small reading groups in one of two ways:

1. Members of a group read the same novel.
2. Each member of a group reads different selections by the same author, or books that explore a similar theme or genre.

Reading groups can be formed according to criteria such as:

- Homogeneous abilities
- Heterogeneous abilities
- Social skills
- Interests
- Gender
- Random selection

Ideally, teachers organize groups in response to students' learning needs and common interests. They might re-organize the groups often to refresh the discussions and to expose students to multiple perspectives. By collaborating regularly in pairs and in small groups, students develop the interpersonal skills necessary to share ideas, responses, and emotional reactions with one another as they progress through a novel.

Independent Reading   Devote at least 15 to 20 minutes of class time per day to independent reading. Successful independent reading depends on an extensive selection of novels in the classroom and/or in local libraries. In becoming independent readers, students benefit from observing how others, including the teacher, select novels based on their individual reading interests and then share their reactions to their reading.

The following chart outlines the strengths and challenges offered by each approach to organizing a novel program.

	STRENGTHS	CHALLENGES
Whole Class	Minimal organization is required Before, during, and after responses are easy to manage Student progress is relatively easy to monitor and assess	No individual student choice is permitted The diversity of readers' abilities and interests is not addressed Students cannot pace the reading experience for themselves
Small Groups	Only a small number of novels in a set are required Groups can be organized by gender, interests, and ability Rich interactive response opportunities are provided	Careful monitoring is needed to ensure that all groups stay on task Students need prior experience of collaboration within a group The teacher must balance group interaction with instruction
Independent Reading	Students enjoy choosing their own material to read Individual needs and interests are accommodated Only one copy of a book per student is required	The teacher must ensure that all students are reading deeply Each student's reading progress must be tracked The teacher must monitor and assess a wide range of reading behaviors and responses

Celebrating Novels

To round out a novel program, readers can participate in activities that promote and celebrate the novels they've read. For example, students can display their book reviews on a class bulletin board or in the school foyer. They can script and role-play a mock radio or television interview with a favorite author.

Through response activities, readers confirm that they have understood what they have read and they make links to their own life experiences. They develop their own identities as active, engaged readers as they select a form of response that reflects their individual learning styles. Choosing from a wide range of multi-sensory response activities helps readers develop self-confidence and critical thinking skills. Some possibilities include response journals, literature circles, book talks, e-mail chat groups, art, drama, and multimedia presentations such as PowerPoint®. Graphic organizers are powerful tools in helping students plan their response activities (see pages 16 to 23).

Thinking About…Celebrating Novels
- What can we accomplish by engaging in activities that promote and celebrate novels?
- What are some of your favorite ways to respond to novels?

2. ORGANIZING A NOVEL PROGRAM

Guidelines for Choosing Novels

Generally, we tend to choose novels that appeal to our needs and interests and that broaden our views of the world. Ask your friends or family members to recommend novels they've enjoyed and recommend your favorite titles to them in return. If your classroom is not well stocked with novels, check out the school library, the public library, new and used bookstores, and perhaps book clubs. You can exchange novels with friends or classmates. Have fun selecting lots of novels for independent reading and for your own personal collection.

Guidelines for the Teacher

- Provide students with an array of novels from which to choose.
- Stock novels that vary by topic, by author, and by level of difficulty.
- Display books in inviting and imaginative ways and find ways to advertise and promote a wide variety of titles.
- Survey students' needs, interests, and favorite topics and take these into account when recommending novels to them.
- Read aloud part or all of a novel, and recommend other books written on the same theme or by the same author.
- Encourage students to take time to browse through libraries and bookstores.
- Share opinions about novels and writers expressed by your peers, librarians, and reviewers.
- Outline potential response activities for novels.
- Create lots of opportunities for students to talk about their favorite authors and titles.

Guidelines for the Student

- Take time to browse freely and to make personal choices from the classroom novel collection as well as from other sources.
- Read a number of books by the same author or books on a theme that you find exciting.
- Ask friends, classmates, a teacher, a librarian, or family members who know your interests and abilities to advise you about novels they think you would enjoy.
- Feel comfortable in your reading tastes and choices. You do not have to defend your reading preferences!
- Keep a log of the novels you have read (including title, author, topic, and what you liked or didn't like about the story).
- Don't hesitate to abandon a novel you are not enjoying!

Factors Influencing the Novels We Choose

Level of Difficulty   On a flip test, does the novel seem too easy? Too challenging?

Cover   Are the title and cover art enticing? Does the back cover blurb make the story sound exciting?

Format   Is the book paperback or hardcover? Do you find the print easy to read? Does the novel seem too long? Too short? Do you like the length of the chapters? Are there any illustrations?

Author   Is the author a popular writer who is familiar to you or someone new whose work you'd like to explore?

Series   Do you like to read about the adventures of a favorite character? Or do you prefer new characters and situations?

Setting   Is the setting modern or historical? Is the story set in the future or in another country? Does the setting strike you as familiar or exotic?

Interest   As you flip through the book, do the story and characters catch your interest? Will your curiosity about a topic be satisfied by reading this book?

Availability   Can you locate the book you want in your classroom, school resource center, or local library? Will you have to buy or borrow a copy?

Reading Context   Will you read the book on your own or in a group?

Issues   What will you learn about personal, social, and political conflicts by reading the novel?

Cultures   What will you learn about your own cultural identity or the cultural identities of other people by reading the novel?

Genre   Is the genre familiar to you? Is this your typical choice?

Popularity   Is the book popular with other students?

Gender Appeal   Is the protagonist male or female? Does the book seem free of stereotypes?

Recommendations   Has the book been recommended by a teacher? A family member? A friend? A librarian? A bookstore owner?

Cost   Can you afford to buy the book if it's not available in your school or local library?

Thinking About…Choosing Novels

- How do you choose novels to read?
- What do you think most influences someone's choice of novel?
- How many best-selling authors have you read?
- In your reading journal, tell in your own words what traits or qualities might make a novelist successful.

3. CHOOSING NOVELS

Overview of Genres

Many types of novels have been written over the centuries, and sometimes writers like to experiment with new forms. For example, graphic novels (in both print and film versions) have become popular in recent years. As the illustration shows, novel genres range from pure fantasy set in completely imaginary worlds to highly realistic novels based on real events. Many genres feature a mixture of fantasy and realism.

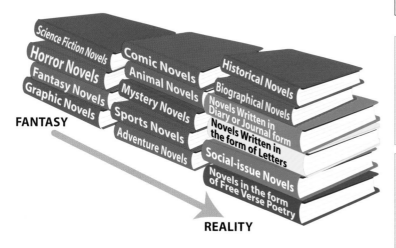

How many of the genres shown in the illustration have you read? Copy the chart below into your notebook and complete it to find out. Then compare your chart with a peer's and talk about why you are drawn to particular genres of novels. What new genres would you like to explore?

Genres I Have Read (include sample titles)	Genres I Have Never Read	Genres I Might Like to Try

Thinking About…Choosing Genres

- Which genres are most familiar to you? Why do you think this is so?
- Which new genres might you like to try reading? Briefly explain your choices.

Thinking About…Favorite Titles

- What top ten novels would you recommend for your grade?
- What are the best titles you'd recommend for boys? For girls?

Authors Hall of Fame for Novel Readers

Grades 4 to 6

Lloyd Alexander
Natalie Babbitt
Betsy Byars
Matt Christopher
Beverly Cleary
Andrew Clements
Eoin Colfer
Karen Cushman
Roald Dahl
Kate DiCamillo
Deborah Ellis
Cynthia de Felice
Louise Fitzhugh
Paul Fleischman
Ralph Fletcher
Jean Fritz
Jack Gantos
John Reynolds Gardiner
Patricia Reilly Giff
Morris Gleitzman
Andy Griffiths
Kevin Henkes
James Howe
Dick King-Smith

Brian Jacques
E. L. Konigsburg
Gail Carson Levine
C. S. Lewis
Jean Little
Anne M. Martin
Lucy Maude Montgomery
Phyllis Reynolds Naylor
Barbara Park
Daniel Manus Pinkwater
Cynthia Rylant
Louis Sachar
Jon Scieszka
Richard Scrimger
Tor Siedler
Donald J. Sobol
William Steig
Mildred Taylor
Wendelin Van Draanen
Cynthia Voight
Laura Ingalls Wilder
Eric Wilson

Grades 4 to 9

Avi
Judy Blume
Sharon Creech
Christopher Paul Curtis
Paula Danziger
Gordon Korman
Lois Lowry
Katherine Paterson
Gary Paulsen
Richard Peck
J. K. Rowling
Jerry Spinelli
Eric Walters
Jacqueline Wilson

Grades 7 to 9

David Almond
Laurie Halse Anderson
Ann Brashares
Bruce Brooks
Susan Cooper
Robert Cormier
Chris Crutcher
Brian Doyle
Lois Duncan
Anne Fine
Sheree Fitch
Paula Fox
Karen Hesse
S. E. Hinton
Monica Hughes
M. E. Kerr
Ron Koertge
Ursula LeGuin
Robert Lipsyte
Kevin Major
Anne McCaffrey
Farley Mowat
Walter Dean Myers
Donna Jo Napoli

Joan Lowery Nixon
Joyce Carol Oates
Kenneth Oppel
Francine Pascal
Kit Pearson
Rodman Philbrick
Tamora Pierce
Philip Pullman
William Sleator
Mildred Taylor
J. R. R. Tolkien
Tim Wynne-Jones
Jane Yolen
Paul Zindel

Top Ten Lists

Ten Novels for the Teacher to Read Aloud

Skellig by David Almond
The End of the Beginning by Avi
Tuck Everlasting by Natalie Babbitt
Weasel by Cynthia de Felice
Stone Fox by John Reynolds Gardiner
The Music of Dolphins by Karen Hesse
Kira-Kira by Cynthia Kadohata
Touching Spirit Bear by Ben Mikaelsen
A Single Shard by Linda Sue Park
The Young Man and the Sea by Rodman
  Philbrick (see also *Freak the Mighty*; *Max
  the Mighty*)

Ten Great Novels, Grades 4 – 6

Love That Dog by Sharon Creech (see also
  Heartbeat)
The Tale of Despereaux by Kate DiCamillo
  (see also *Because of Wynn-Dixie*; *The Tiger
  Rising*)
The Breadwinner (trilogy) by Deborah Ellis
  (see also *The Heaven Shop*)
*Mable Riley: A Reliable Record of Humdrum
  Peril and Romance* by Marthe Jocelyn
Shiloh (trilogy) by Phyllis Reynolds Naylor
Silverwing (trilogy) by Kenneth Oppel

Bridge to Terabithia by Katherine Paterson
  (see also *The Flip-Flop Girl*; *Jip: His Story*)
The Crazy Man by Pamela Porter
Loser by Jerry Spinelli (see also *Crash*; *Maniac
  Magee*; *Wringer*)
Run by Eric Walters (see also *I've Got an Idea*;
  Trapped in Ice)

Ten Great Novels, Grades 7 – 9

The House of Scorpions by Nancy Farmer
The Gravesavers by Sheree Fitch
Out of the Dust by Karen Hesse (see also
  Witness; *Aleutian Sparrow*)
The Giver by Lois Lowry (see also *Gathering
  Blue*; *The Messenger*)
Daniel's Story by Carol Matas
Monster by Walter Dean Myers (see also
  Shooter)
Airborn by Kenneth Oppel (sequel:
  Skybreaker)
Milkweed by Jerry Spinelli
Chanda's Secrets by Allan Stratton
A Thief in the House of Memory by Tim
  Wynne-Jones (see also *The Maestro*)

Series for Novel Readers, Grades 4 – 6

The Adventures of Eddie Dickens by Philip
  Ardagh
Molly Moon by Georgia Byng

The Spiderwick Chronicles by Holly Black and
  Tony DiTerlizzi
On the Run by Gordon Korman
The Chronicles of Narnia by C. S. Lewis
The Amazing Days of Abby Hayes by Anne
  Mazer
The Time Warp Trio by Jon Scieszka
A Series of Unfortunate Events by Lemony
  Snicket
Geronimo Stilton by Geronimo Stilton
Shredderman: Secret Identity by Wendelin Van
  Draanen

Series for Novel Readers, Grades 6 – 9

Animorphs by K. A. Applegate
The Sisterhood of the Traveling Pants by Ann
  Brashares
Warriors by Evan Hunter
Tales of Redwall by Brian Jacques
Pendragon by D. J. MacHale
Hatchet by Gary Paulsen
Protector of the Small Quartet by Tamora
  Pierce
Septimus Heap by Angie Sage
The Edge Chronicles by Paul Stewart and
  Chris Riddell
Goosebumps by R. L. Stine

Ten Great Graphic Novels

The Hobbit by Dixon Chuck
Hikaru No Go (series) by Yumi Hotta
Meridian by Barbara Kessel
Knights of the Zodiac (series) by Masami Kurumada
Castle Waiting (series) by Linda Medley
The Adventures of Captain Underpants (series) by Dav Pilkey
Frankenstein by Gary Reed
Bone: Out from Boneville by Jeff Smith (see also *The Great Cow Race*)
Shaman King (series) by Hiroyuki Takei
Prince of Tennis (series) by Konomi Takeshi

If you liked *Harry Potter* by J. K. Rowling…

The Book of Three (series) by Lloyd Alexander
The Book Without Words by Avi (see also *Crispin*)
Artemis Fowl by Eoin Colfer
The City of Ember by Jeanne Du Prau (sequel: *The People of Sparks*)
The Thief Lord by Cornelia Funke (see also *Dragon Rider*; *Inkheart*; *Inkspell*)
Coraline by Neil Gaiman
Sabriel by Garth Nix (sequels: *Lirael*; *Abhorsen*)
Eragon by Christopher Paolini (sequel: *Eldest*)
The Golden Compass (trilogy) by Philip Pullman

The Bartimaeus Trilogy by Jonathan Stroud

If you liked *Holes* by Louis Sachar…

Dear Mr. Henshaw by Beverly Cleary (sequel: *Strider*)
Bud, Not Buddy by Christopher Paul Curtis
Spider Boy by Ralph Fletcher (see also *Fig Pudding*; *Flying Solo*)
Joey Pigza Swallowed the Key (trilogy) by Jack Gantos
Hoot by Carl Hiaasen (see also *Flush*)
When Zachary Beaver Came to Town by Kimberly Willis Holt
No More Dead Dogs by Gordon Korman
Feather Boy by Nicky Singer
Maniac Magee by Jerry Spinelli
The Lottie Project by Jacqueline Woodson (see also *The Worry Website*; *Secrets*)

If you liked *Zombie Buts from Uranus* (trilogy) by Andy Griffiths…

The Twits by Roald Dahl (see also *Matilda*; *The BFG*)
The Giggler Treatment by Roddy Doyle
A Barrel of Laughs / A Vale of Tears by Jules Feiffer (see also *A Room With a Zoo*)
This Can't Be Happening at MacDonald Hall (series) by Gordon Korman
Fat Men from Outer Space by Daniel Pinkwater

Jacob Two-Two Meets the Hooded Fang (trilogy) by Mordecai Richler
Sideways Stories From a Wayside School by Louis Sachar
The Nose From Jupiter by Richard Scrimger (see also *The Boy from Earth*; *Noses are Red*)
Mean Margaret by Tor Siedler
Barry, Boyhound by Andy Spearman

If you liked *The Outsiders* by S. E. Hinton…

Speak by Laurie Halse Anderson
Bucking the Sarge by Christopher Paul Curtis
Inventing Elliot by Graham Gardner
Shattering Glass by Gail Giles
Slake's Limbo by Felice Holman
The Misfits by James Howe (see also *Totally Joe*)
The Insiders by J. Minter
Autobiography of My Dead Brother by Walter Dean Myers
The Girl Who Owned a City by O. T. Nelson
Stars by Eric Walters (see also *Diamonds in the Rough*; *Visions*)

Making Sense of the Novels We Read

Before reading a novel we have chosen, we can

- think about the novel's title, examine the cover art, and read the blurb on the back cover or on the inside cover flaps;
- skim the text for an idea of the novel's content and structure;
- prepare ourselves for reading by drawing upon our prior knowledge of the novel's main topic(s).

During reading, we can build a coherent, personal interpretation of the novel by

- searching for the most important ideas;
- anticipating what will happen next in the story;
- reading ahead for additional context clues;
- rereading to clarify a part of the text that confuses us or to relate new knowledge to existing knowledge;
- creating mental images to visualize an object or event described in the novel;
- looking for interconnecting details;
- monitoring our reading to ensure comprehension.

After reading, we can

- reflect on and talk about what we have read;
- relate what we have read to our own experiences;
- respond to the text in a variety of ways to enrich and extend the meaning-making process.

Reading Comprehension Strategies

Effective readers apply a range of strategies to construct meaning and to clarify understanding as they read. Teachers model the use of a particular strategy or strategies first. Then readers practice applying the strategy when they interact with text. Read the passage below and then consider the purpose of the questions on the following page

It was in the year 1046, on a cold winter's night, when a fog, thick as wool and dank as a dead man's hand, crept up from the River Scrogg into the ancient town of Fulworth. The fog settled like an ice shroud over the town, filling the mud-clogged streets and crooked lanes from Westgate to Bishopsgate, from Three Rats Quay upon the decaying riverbanks to Saint Osyth's Cathedral by the city centre. It clung to the crumbling walls. It heightened the stench of rotten hay and offal, of vinegary wine and rancid ale. It muffled the sound of pealing church bells calling the weary faithful to apprehensive prayers.

In a neglected corner of town, at the bottom of Clutterbuck Lane, with its grimy courtyard and noxious well, against the town's walls, stood a dilapidated two-story house. The first level windows were blocked up with stone. A single second-floor window was curtained.

Excerpted from *The Book Without Words: A Fable of Medieval Magic* by Avi (New York, NY: Hyperion Books for Children, 2005)

Activating prior knowledge: *Ask yourself, "What do I know about this topic? What does this remind me of?"* **Example:** What do you know about life in medieval times?

Making predictions: *Use your prior knowledge and personal experience to guess might happen in the novel.* **Example:** What do you think this novel is going to be about?

Visualizing: *Use descriptive words and phrases and vivid images to create pictures in your mind.* **Example:** If this were the opening scene in a movie, what images might you expect to see?

Questioning: *Ask questions such as "I wonder what 'offal' means? I wonder if my teacher or a classmate can tell me the meaning?"* **Example:** What questions do you have about the story?

Drawing inferences: *Use stated and implied messages to reach a new and deeper understanding of the text.* **Example:** How has the author conveyed a mysterious, sinister mood in this introduction?

Finding important ideas: *Determine the most important ideas based on clues in the language and details provided in the text.* **Example:** What words or phrases tell you that the setting is a poor town?

Summarizing: *Combine meanings, delete less important details, and condense the key messages to restate the text in your own words.* **Example:** Rewrite this introduction in one or two sentences.

Synthesizing: *Combine ideas or information to reach a conclusion.* **Example:** How has the information in the introduction helped you understand that this is a "Medieval fable"?

Monitoring and Revising Comprehension: *Interrupt your reading if you lose track of the meaning and use a "fix-it" strategy such as slowing down your pace or rereading to help you continue.* **Example:** What words or phrases were unfamiliar to you? What did you do to understand the text?

Evaluating: *Make judgements based on a thoughtful analysis of the text.* **Example:** How successfully has the author captured your interest in this introduction?

Thinking About…the Strategies We Use as Readers

- Identify several different comprehension strategies that you currently use as you read.
- What might you do when you read something that is difficult or challenging?

4. READING FOR COMPREHENSION

Using Graphic Organizers

Graphic organizers such as charts, webs, and Venn diagrams can help us process information. These tools help us focus on important concepts and how these concepts are interrelated. Graphic organizers enable readers to identify, recall, and organize details, ideas, and relationships in a simple visual format.

Predictions Chart

Use a chart like the one below to record predictions as you read each chapter or section of a novel.

BEFORE READING What I predict will happen in each chapter/section...	AFTER READING What I know now...
Chapter _____	
Chapter _____	

New Word Chart

Use a three-column chart to list unfamiliar words you encounter as you read a novel. For each word, record your guess as to what the word means based on the words around it before searching for the word in a dictionary. In the third column, record the dictionary definition.

New Word	My Guess	Dictionary Definition

Character Web

In the centre **circle**, write a character's name. In each **oval**, list words that describe the character's personality traits. In each **rectangle**, describe a behavior that demonstrates the personality trait.

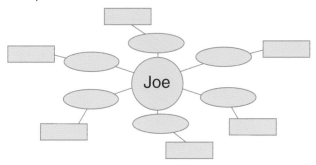

Joe

T-Chart

Compare two characters from the same novel, two characters from different novels, or a character's life to your own life. Include details such as physical appearance, personality traits, social relationships, and accomplishments.

[Name of character]'s Life	My Life

Road Map

As you "travel" through a novel, record important incidents and places where these events occur on a simple road map. You can use words and/or pictures to record the novel's settings.

Plot Outline

1. Place your hand palm-down with your fingers spread out on a blank piece of paper. Trace around your hand. On each finger in your drawing, list an exciting event from the novel.

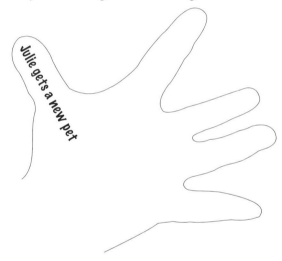

2. In the space between each finger, list an event that you think is important but less exciting than those listed on the fingers. You now have a total of nine events.
3. Compare your outline with one drawn by someone who read the same novel.

Novel Pyramid

Use an outline like the one shown below to summarize a novel in 36 words. When you have finished, find a partner who completed a pyramid on the same book. Compare and discuss your choices.

1 word that explains the theme of the novel
2 words that express your opinion of the novel
3 words that describe the setting
4 words that describe the main character
5 characters' names
6 new words you learned by reading the novel
7 words that summarize the main problem at the heart of the novel
8 words that summarize the plot

5. PROCESSING INFORMATION

Purpose of Response Activities

Responding to a novel is as important as reading the novel. When readers express their personal responses to literature freely, they demonstrate their growth as literate learners. They can talk about a novel, read dialogue aloud, illustrate scenes from the novel, or construct models of settings in a novel. They can role-play characters and events. They can also write their own material based on ideas sparked by a novel. Additionally, they can read other novels in the same genre or by the same author. With the teacher's guidance, collaborative responses can extend each reader's personal response and help generate a wider and more thoughtful understanding of the story.

Usually, response activities involve *doing* something based on what has been read. Response activities can take the form of discussion, writing, drama, or art. When we engage in response activities, whether on our own or with others, we are invited to go beyond the text. Response activities encourage readers to relate concepts in the novel to their own experiences, and to tap into memories and insights elicited by the intensity of the reading experience.

Response activities allow readers to "open up" the text for discussion. By responding in a format that suits their learning style, students can reflect on the whole experience of reading the novel and they can expand or modify their understanding. Response activities encourage readers to voice their viewpoints and opinions. They become aware that opinions that are relevant to but not necessarily identical with those in the novel are equally valid. As readers articulate their interpretations of a novel and learn from exposure to differing viewpoints, knowledge, and experience, they begin to appreciate the complexities of a well-written novel. They begin to pay attention to the appropriateness and effectiveness of choice of words, ideas, style, and other features of writing. When readers respond to the novels they have read, they begin to explore in greater depth the traditional elements of literature – plot, characterization, setting, theme, and style.

Critical Literacy

Reflective readers also learn to look beyond the surface message, to read between the lines, and to recognize that no text is neutral. They learn to question the authority of texts and to examine issues of bias and perspective. By reading widely, they see how novels reflect the choices, positions, and beliefs of the authors who created them. They come to understand that authors construct their texts with the goal of influencing the reader in some way. Put another way, readers develop and practice critical literacy skills.

Response activities extend and enrich each reader's interaction with the text. Ideally, response activities:

- invite a careful, analytical reading of a novel through the lens of critical literacy;
- expand the reader's knowledge of a topic or topics;
- clarify initial understandings of a novel;
- help readers discover new patterns of thinking; and
- promote interaction and collaboration with others.

Types of Responses

Responding Orally

Book talks can be as informal as two or three friends meeting to discuss a novel that one or both readers have read. They can be as formal as a whole class discussion in which everyone discusses a novel they have read or heard the teacher read aloud. Some discussions can be tape-recorded and shared with others. Sharing thoughts and feelings with classmates who have read the same novels can lead to more sophisticated literary generalizations and deeper understanding.

The Importance of Talk

In small groups, discussion is often spontaneous. Group members offer their comments, concerns, and criticisms in response to what they have read. Before reading, group members can gather to predict, anticipate, and set the stage for the novel's narrative. During and after reading, they can engage in purposeful talk to construct both personal and collective meaning.

Talk can also be the starting point for a variety of response activities. Such activities might include research, role-playing, storytelling, brainstorming, questioning, writing, and reading aloud. As we dig inside a novel's narrative, we can revise our understanding and create our own stories in light of what others reveal as they attempt to make meaning as well.

Ten Contexts for Book Talks

1. A student interviews another student about a novel he or she has read.
2. Pairs or small groups share opinions or enthusiasms about parts of a novel, or the novel as a whole.
3. Students consult with others to plan and prepare a response activity.
4. Students form small groups to discuss a novel that all group members have read. (Students may need the teacher's help in devising a framework for their discussion.)
5. In a small group, in which the teacher is a member, students discuss a novel that everyone has read.
6. The teacher leads a large group discussion about a novel that has been read aloud to the class.
7. A student and teacher can share reactions, ask and answer questions, and make connections during a reading conference.
8. Students tell stories that come to mind as they read the novel. These stories can focus on events that have happened in their own lives or in the lives of others, or they can reflect events in the media.
9. Students meet with others who have not read the same novel to retell events and share reactions.
10. Students meet in literature circles, taking on a role to discuss what they've read.

Responding in Writing

Well-written novels provide readers with the best possible models of narrative writing – real books written with real intent for real audiences. When reading a novel, we learn a great deal about the craft of writing. The author of the novel can often serve as an excellent writing teacher, and students can:

- observe how writers represent experience
- borrow vocabulary for their own writing
- learn how to describe characters and setting
- understand how to emphasize what is significant in terms of plot
- learn to present factual information and to inform readers of the main idea

Ten Ways to Write About Our Reading

1. **Jot reactions** to a novel on sticky notes, in response journals, or on personal copies of the book.
2. **Add entries** to a cumulative class response chart (e.g., to showcase new vocabulary or key questions that were raised).
3. **Write a letter** to a teacher, friend, or family member about a book.
4. **List questions** that come to mind for further discussion.
5. **Record book-talk** conversations.
6. **Describe** a novel's events, characters, settings, and conflicts.
7. **Retell** the story as newspaper articles, fictitious letters, or diary entries.
8. **Create a Readers Theatre script** that focuses on one section or chapter of a novel.
9. **Write in role** as a character that appears in the novel (e.g., create a character's diary entry, a letter to a relative, or a fictitious autobiography).
10. **Share opinions** of the novel in a book review that others can read.

Reading Response Journals

A reading response journal (also called a dialogue journal or a literature log) is a convenient and flexible tool to help readers reflect on their reading. Keeping a journal permits readers to communicate and explore the ideas and feelings that a novel evokes, and to relate what they read to their own lives.

It's fun and informative to share journals with others. A teacher, friend, or family member who reads selected entries can begin a dialogue with the reader by offering comments on their responses, pointing out connections with their thinking, and expressing their viewpoints.

When a trusted audience responds to the journal in a conversation, readers can clarify their thinking about the story, raise questions to explore further, or make connections with their own lives. A reading response journal fosters a connection between reading and writing.

Reading response journals place readers at the centre of their learning. These journals can serve as a record of the reader's thinking about literature and of his or her reactions as readers. They prompt learners to reflect on, interact with, and find personal meaning in works of literature. They encourage storytelling, questioning, imagining, and speculating.

A journal provides ongoing information about readers' thinking and learning – for students as readers and for teachers as audience and guide. A reading response journal is a powerful way to stimulate interaction among teacher, text, and learner.

Journal Prompts

The following sample journal prompts can help students reflect on their reading as they record their responses:

1. What are you enjoying/not enjoying about the novel?
2. What, if anything, puzzles you as you read the novel?
3. Is the novel easy or hard to read? Do you sometimes reread parts?
4. During your reading, do you "see" the story in your mind?
5. What problems emerge in the novel? How do you think these problems will be resolved?
6. What words, phrases, or sentences made an impression on you?
7. What interests you about the character(s) in the novel?
8. What advice would you give to one of the characters in the novel?
9. What advice would you give to the author of the novel?
10. How do you feel about the way the author told the story?
11. Have you or someone you know experienced events similar to the ones that took place in the novel?
12. What did the novel make you wonder about?
13. What is the author's overall message?
14. Do you think the novel's title is appropriate?
15. What will you tell your friends about this novel?

Responding Through Art

Many readers enjoy representing their responses visually. By drawing, painting, making models, or constructing collages, students – especially visual learners – can convey their thoughts and feelings about a novel they've read.

For various reasons, including anxiety or difficulties with language, some readers are unable to respond orally or in writing. For these students, visual arts can offer a non-threatening opportunity to express their understanding and appreciation of a novel and its elements. Illustrations and other art projects can serve as artifacts for group discussion and can help others understand what a reader is "saying" about the novel through the details, style, and emotions represented in the piece of art. Try some of the following ideas.

Design a character's room showing furniture, books, souvenirs, and posters that represent the character's personality, interests, hobbies, and possessions.

Imagine you have been hired as an artist to **create illustrations** for a novel you have read. Which scenes painted a vivid picture in your mind? Which medium will you use to communicate your ideas?

Create a portrait mask for a character from a novel you've read. If you wish, cut out pictures from magazines or newspapers to represent events or symbols that reveal something about the character.

Film producers commission storyboards to help them structure the scenes in a film before it is shot. **Create a storyboard** showing a series of sketches representing plot highlights of one chapter or section of a novel. Your sketches could represent the most powerful images that you would see if this novel were made into a film.

Imagine that a novel you have read is going to be made into a play or a film. The director has hired you to construct a set representing rooms or places described in the novel. **Construct a model set** for a scene in your novel.

Responding Through Drama

Drama provides opportunities to step into the shoes of a character and to gain a better understanding of the character's dilemmas. By responding to literature through drama, readers can express a character's innermost thoughts and explore a story from a variety of viewpoints, both orally and in writing.

The conflicts that arise in a novel can provide meaningful opportunities to work with others – in role and out of role – to solve problems, make decisions, and re-enact significant events. Even if the context is remote from the readers' experience in time or place, students can respond through drama to examine a character's actions, relationships, and predicaments. By improvising a situation portrayed in a novel, we respond as if the events created by the author are real and we step inside the author's fictitious world.

The text of the novel can also provide sources for dramatic interpretation. Readers can use narration and dialogue to develop scripts, monologues, or Readers Theatre presentations.

Imagine that you can talk on the phone with a character from a novel. What questions might you ask? What advice would you give? Work with a partner to **improvise a conversation** between the character and a friend, relative, or another character from the novel.

With a small group of peers who have read and enjoyed the same novel, choose a scene to dramatize. Decide on how the text will be narrated and how members of the group will role-play the characters in order to **create a dramatic presentation** of the scene from the novel.

Imagine that the characters in the novel you have read keep a journal. Pretend that you are one of the characters and **write a fictitious journal entry** (or series of entries) that would reveal the character's thoughts and attitudes to events or relationships depicted in the novel.

Choose an interesting section of the novel that features dialogue (minimum one-half page). Working in a group, **transform this dialogue into a written script** to be performed by others. How many characters will you need? How will you handle narration?

Imagine that a character in a novel you've read is having dreams about a problem he or she is facing or about a past event (either troubling or pleasing). Work in a group to **create a dream** that reveals something important about the character and the story's conflict. You can use music, movement (including slow motion), dance, sound effects, still images, or props.

Thinking About…Responding to Novels

- Describe the most innovative way in which you've responded to a novel. What made the activity especially creative?
- What might be a unique way to respond to a novel when working in a small group? In a large group?

PROFESSIONAL READING

Allen, Janet. *Yellow Brick Roads: Shared and Guided Paths to Independent Reading 4 – 12*. Portland, ME: Stenhouse Publishers, 2000.

Beers, Kylene. *When Kids Can't Read: What Teachers Can Do*. Portsmouth, NH: Heinemann, 2003.

Booth, David. *Reading and Writing in the Middle Years*. Markham, ON: Pembroke Publishers, 2001.

Booth, David, Joan Green, and Jack Booth. *I Want to Read!: Reading, Writing and Really Learning*. Oakville, ON: Rubicon Publishing; Toronto, ON: Thomson Nelson Publishing, 2004.

Daniels, Harvey. *Literature Circles: Voice and Choice in the Student-centred Classroom*. Markham, ON: Pembroke Publishers/Portland, ME: Stenhouse Publishers, 2002.

Harvey, Stephanie and Anne Goudvis. *Strategies That Work: Teaching Comprehension to Enhance Understanding*. Portland, ME: Stenhouse Publishers, 2000.

Kropp, Paul. *How to Make Your Child a Reader for Life*. Toronto, ON: Random House, 2000.

Kuta, Katherine Wiesolek and Susan Zernial. *Novel Ideas for Young Readers*. Englewood, CO: Teacher Ideas Press, 2000.

Marshall, Jodi Crum. *Are They Really Reading? Extending SSR in the Middle Grades*. Portland, ME: Stenhouse Publishers, 2002.

Setterington, Ken and Deidre Baker. *A Guide to Canadian Children's Books in English*. Toronto, ON: McClelland & Stewart, 2003.

Sibberson, Franki and Karen Szymusiak. *Still Learning to Read: Teaching Students to Read in Grades 3 – 6*. Portland, ME: Stenhouse Publishers, 2000.

Swartz, Larry and David Booth. *Literacy Techniques: For Building Successful Readers and Writers*. Markham, ON: Pembroke Publishers, 2004.

MY PROFILE AS A READER OF NOVELS

Name: _____ Date: _____

1. I like to read novels that _____

_____

2. I don't like to read novels that _____

_____

3. The best novels I've ever read are _____

_____

4. My favorite author of novels is _____

5. My favorite novel genre is _____

6. I usually finish a novel in about _____ (days/ weeks)

7. I'd like to read more novels about _____

_____

8. One way I have grown as a reader by reading novels is _____

_____

9. Some interesting things I learned from reading novels are _____

_____

10. For the next month, my personal novel-reading goals are _____

_____

_____

READING OBSERVATION CHECKLIST

Name _____

STUDENT READING BEHAVIORS	Scale (lowest)	1	2	3	4	5	(highest)
Appears to enjoy reading novels		❑	❑	❑	❑	❑	
Reads voluntarily		❑	❑	❑	❑	❑	
Attempts to finish novels		❑	❑	❑	❑	❑	
Can choose novels independently		❑	❑	❑	❑	❑	
Chooses from a wide variety of novels		❑	❑	❑	❑	❑	
Reads more than one novel by the same author		❑	❑	❑	❑	❑	
Enjoys reading novels in a series		❑	❑	❑	❑	❑	
Uses the school and/or community library		❑	❑	❑	❑	❑	
Chooses novels appropriate to her/his reading level		❑	❑	❑	❑	❑	
Focuses on meaning when reading		❑	❑	❑	❑	❑	
Is willing to read challenging novels		❑	❑	❑	❑	❑	
Has favorite novels		❑	❑	❑	❑	❑	
Enjoys listening to novels read aloud		❑	❑	❑	❑	❑	

STUDENT RESPONSES TO NOVELS		1	2	3	4	5	
Retells stories		❑	❑	❑	❑	❑	
Contributes to class discussions		❑	❑	❑	❑	❑	
Talks about novels with peers		❑	❑	❑	❑	❑	
Writes about novels		❑	❑	❑	❑	❑	
Can respond in role		❑	❑	❑	❑	❑	
Interprets aspects of the novel through art or other non-print media		❑	❑	❑	❑	❑	
Asks thoughtful questions about the novel		❑	❑	❑	❑	❑	
Relates novels to personal experiences		❑	❑	❑	❑	❑	
Expresses opinions and demonstrates critical thinking		❑	❑	❑	❑	❑	
Chooses response activities independently		❑	❑	❑	❑	❑	
Chooses activities that focus on various aspects of the novel		❑	❑	❑	❑	❑	

TEN QUESTIONS TO ASK ABOUT A NOVEL

1. If one of the characters from your novel registered in your school, how well might the character fit in?

   _____

   _____

2. If you were to make a film of this story, what scene(s) might you skip if you couldn't feature them all? Why?

   _____

   _____

3. Why do you think the author wrote this novel? Who do you think might be interested in reading this novel?

   _____

   _____

4. What might you tell someone about this novel – in exactly 50 words?

   _____

   _____

5. What is one event that happened in this story that reminded you of an event in your own life or in the life of someone you know?

   _____

   _____

6. Do you think this story needs an epilogue to explain what happens to the characters after the novel ends? What do you think the future holds for each character?

   _____

   _____

7. Is the title appropriate for this novel? If not, suggest alternative titles.

   _____

   _____

8. Which sentence, paragraph, or section made a vivid impression on your imagination? Create an illustration that would represent this text.

   _____

   _____

9. How might aspects of this novel change if the main characters were of the opposite gender?

   _____

   _____

10. How did this novel help you grow as a reader?

   _____

   _____

INDEPENDENT READING PROFILE

Title of Book _____

Author _____ Number of pages _____

1. a) When did you start reading the novel? _____

    b) When did you finish reading the novel? _____

2. On a scale from 1 to 10 (highest), how would you rate this novel?
    Explain your rating.

    1   2   3   4   5   6   7   8   9   10

    _____

    _____

3. Summarize this novel in exactly 25 words.

    _____

    _____

4. Find a sentence or paragraph from this novel that you particularly liked.
    Briefly explain your choice.

    _____

    _____

5. What did you learn by reading this novel?

    _____

    _____

6. What about this novel reminded you of relationships or events in your own life (or
    in the life of someone you know)?

    _____

    _____

7. What are three questions that you would like to ask the author?

    _____

    _____

    _____

MY NOVEL READING THIS YEAR

If you were to list all the novels you have read this year, what would your list look like? Have you read a range of genres? A number of different authors? Did you discover new favorites? Were there some novels you did not finish? If so, why?

Use the chart below to record the novels you've read throughout the school year. If you like, compare your chart with one completed by a friend or a classmate.

TITLE / AUTHOR	GENRE	DATE FINISHED	COMMENTS